# SURVIVING YOU

## A JOURNEY OF SELF DISCOVERY

### SHATERIA. A FRANKLIN

Cover Photo: Mercy Center for Women
Women Making History Portrait by Paul Lorei 2024

I would like to dedicate Surviving You: A Journey of Self Discovery to all the beautiful women around the world who are on journeys searching to find who they are. The women searching for wholeness and oneness. The women who are overcoming their old selves in search of the person they have hopes to become. I pray that this book as helps you along to the way. I hope that you have the ability to stop and look around you often on your journey and soak up whatever moment that you are in. I see you QUEEN, you are fearfully and wonderfully made. You are a force to be reckoned with and the world is waiting for you. WALK proudly in your evolution and continue to evolve each and every day.

I want to thank my husband Marcus for always being what I need in my life at all times. Thank you for our journey of growing and learning daily. I am grateful to do this lifetime with you by my side.

Thank you to my mother Terri who is my backbone and my rock. You make being me easy, you support me and love me through all my endeavors, I would not be able to wear all my many hats without your ever present help and love. I appreciate and adore you mommy.

My beautiful children David, Major & Madisyn, you make my entire world go around. I am so proud to be your mother and I strive daily that you are proud to call me mom. I look forward to helping you grow into the people God created you to be. Each and every book will forever be dedicated to you 3. Love mommy.

# CONTENTS

# SURVIVING YOU

## A JOURNEY OF SELF DISCOVERY

Your new life is going to cost you your old one.

It's going to cost you your comfort zone and your sense of direction.

It's going to cost you relationships and friends.

It's going to cost you being likes and understood. It doesn't matter.

The people who are meant for you are going to meet you on the other side. You're going to build a new comfort zone around the things that actually move you forward. Instead of being liked you're going to be loved. Instead of being understood you're going to be seen.

All you're going to lose is what was built for a person you no longer are.

- Brianna Wiest, The Mountain Is You: Transforming Self- Sabotage into Self Mastery

# PREFACE

On your journey you will experience growing pains, nothing hurts more than leaving behind familiarity to walk into an unknown version of yourself. You may have thoughts of fear, doubt or worry. You may question if you are ready to evolve or even if it is necessary.

If you have been praying for something new, something different then often what we don't recognize is that the nucleus of the new is YOU.

It takes wisdom and courage to know when it is time to shed old things, when it is time to sit that baggage down and when it is time to release, reset and renew.

Sometimes the only thing standing between you and your next chapter is YOU!

There is a saying that "only the strong survive" but we often like to think that it applies only to external forces, however our biggest battle usually comes from within.

We learn to survive in trauma, pain, hurt and bondage so much that our minds become conditioned to that state of surviving. So much so that change becomes so hard because we are attached to what we know.

The journey is no light task and is a necessary part of life to get to what you have been purposed to do on this Earth.

I remember when I began writing this very book and the purpose behind it. I thought to myself I remember growing up and being rooted in love, protection and GOD, but I also remember the pain and fear that came when I wanted to truly walk in who I knew God had called me to be.

I recall all the hard work that came with this evolution. It caused me to reflect back over periods in my life and one very moment stood out to me the most.

Losing my father at 13 very suddenly and unexpectedly caused me a great deal of pain. My normal life had suddenly changed without warning and with confusion.

How do you manage such a sudden change? There is no blueprint however you must just simply survive.

Come with me on the journey of these pages and learn ways to survive your inner most battles so that you can make it to the other side of who you were created to be.

This book is filled with gems and real life experiences of survival and overcoming.

Welcome!

# CHAPTER ONE:

## YOU & ONLY YOU

This self-discovery process can often be long and challenging. It's usually a harsh reality when you begin to understand that you are holding yourself back more than any external force you have every experienced.

Although this may be a hard pill to swallow fortunately there is a cure and that cure is YOU. For me it started when I recognized and decided that I would no longer stand in my own way of getting all that God had promised me.

I began to pull back layers, healing old wounds, stopped being a victim and slave to my past and pain. It took some serious time to get to know me, the real me. Not the person that I thought I was or even the person that I was striving to become, but the person who I was in this current moment along my journey.

The one with all the flaws, the one who still had not faced head on certain trauma, the one who was still very much a work in progress. I took a moment to really get to know her for who she was who she wasn't. I discovered that flaws and all she was a very beautiful and genuine soul however I found that I still had so much work to do. I understood that it would take some extreme honesty and some deep soul searching.

I knew it would require courage to face things that I once buried to dig up and confront. I knew it would take strength to tell people who I loved the most that at one point they had hurt me and that it would be equally important to face the fact that I had cause some hurt to people I loved as well.

During this time some key words stood out to me and they held so much value along my journey.

Those words were: INTEGRITY, ACCOUNTABILTY, and FORGIVENESS AND FAITH.

It wasn't long that I realized these were more than words, these were principles that I needed to live by in order to heal and become the best me that I could possibly become.

This has been no light task. I believe that you never stop working and understanding yourself but it is very important to understand that only YOU can save YOU. No one else can do it for you.

It won't do you any good blaming others and pointing fingers. It is easier to complain about your problem rather than actively seeking solutions but easy won't get you to where you want to me. Easy won't help you find a deeper sense of who you are.

You need to make a wise choice between being a victim or being VICTORIOUS.

Victims are always complaining, always looking at the glass half empty, and often finding the problem in anything. These folks will always come up with reasons that they CAN'T do something. They will highlight the issue, the pain and the challenge. Sometimes they don't even realize that they are doing this because they have subconsciously coded victim in their brain.

When you chose VICTORY. You realize that no matter what the issues are that you will OVERCOME and SUCCEED. You feed your mind positive thoughts. You see the problem and automatically begin to analyze possible solutions. These people don't focus on what they lack but remain open to the fact that even being minimally equipped they are capable of turning nothing into something.

Which person are you? BE HONEST, the key to all of this is to not live in denial but to understand yourself exactly where you are and to live in VICTORY.

By the end of this book you should have all the tools and encouragement to SURVIVE YOU!

I recall being in a place when I did not even recognize me. I was operating from a place of lack and trauma. I had become so accustom to mistreatment that it had become normal. I had made excuses for why I was completely absorbed in this superficial, non-purposeful way of living. The one thing that saved me and remained near and dear to my heart was that I had been born and raised in the church. All my life I had this undying love for the Lord and I knew that I was created to be something great. I knew that my life had value and I knew that love was universal and that I was created in his image and likeliness.

Those were my roots, those were principals that no matter how far I strayed I always held them in the back of my mind.

At the early age of 3 or 4, I was exposed to praying and understanding of God. All things that came back around full circle as an adult and made it easier for me to make the necessary changes to get out of my own way to walk into my purpose rather running from it.

*Proverbs 22:6 (ESV) Train up a child in the way he should go; even when he is old he will not depart from it.*

Sometimes all it takes is for you to want to move forward. The want is sufficient enough for you to begin traveling this new trail. It is not always super complex as we often make it to be. The simple desire in your heart to be a better you is the foundation. It's the framework that stands the test of time. So ask yourself, do I want to be the best version of myself?

The inner work is what is necessary for the strong and firm foundation. Think of a house a pretty exterior is subject to conditions and elements of life and often is damaged and changed. But go deeper into the foundation, a solid foundation is often unchanged, undamaged and unmoved. So think of this journey to self-discovery as building a firm foundation.

So even when you are walking through the fire your core is protected, or when the rain is pouring or even when the sun is shining so bright your inner framework is solid, strong and reliable to carry you through all the phases and changes of life.

The simple desire will lead to making steps forward but that is not all it will require much more than that. You will encounter many different challenges along the way of doing the work. But do not be discouraged, adversity is the best teacher because it causes you to dig deeper and to fight harder.

Forward motion will cause some discomfort, things won't feel as they once did. Your view will change, your thinking will change and grief is often a byproduct of those changes. Your family and friends may not seem to love and support you as they once did. You may find that at some point in this journey you will feel very alone. But these wilderness moments are the most critical ones. In these moments are when you have no choice but to have deep interactions with yourself and no one else. It is when you are alone with yourself and your thoughts that you begin to find clarity.

I encourage you not to run from your wilderness. Many people have a fear of being alone especially when you are unsure about the person that looks back at you in the mirror.

Understand that this may be God just isolating you so that he can gain your focus and attention.

Alone is not always a bad thing so embrace those moments because it all works together for the greater good.

Can I share a few things that I still actively practice and attribute to my successfulness on this journey? As I stated before the journey is ongoing. It's a lifelong marathon because as people we are always changing, growing and learning new things about ourselves.

## Number 1: Changing Your Perception Is Powerful

When I understood that my perception of my situations had power that's when I began to evaluate the way I viewed everything.

So during times of adversity I no longer studied the problem. I stopped pulling myself down with worry and stress but I began to access that maybe the problems I had been facing were necessary changes to clear a path to a better me.

The way that you view things, the way that you think about things are powerful keys into unlocking doors inside of yourself that you didn't even know existed?

You can poison your whole body with what you allow yourself to THINK.

Stop allowing yourself to have negative thoughts. Transforming your mind will ultimately transform your life.

I encourage you to do this. Each time you are faced with a problem or something is not going right just think of the flipside of it?

For example:

*Your job is stressing you out; at least you have a job.*

*Having a bad day; at least you are alive to even experience what they day brings.*

As referenced before looking at the glass half full vs. half empty.

How you handle something small is how you will handle something big.

These small but necessary foundational steps will help you to deal with the deeper and traumatic experiences that will come throughout life. Because unfortunately we all will experience pain, grief, trauma and uncertainty in more than one way in our life span but it is the way in which we think and our foundational framework that will determine if we sink or swim.

Let me be clear I am no therapist and I am no certified expert but I am a women, a black women that has been through a tremendous amount of death, a substantial amount of pain; physical, mental and spiritual. But I have DONE THE WORK to become the BEST me.

I made a decision that those things would not determine who I was or what my future would hold. I made a CHOICE and while it was not always easy it's been proven to be the best and most necessary choices to get me to where I am in this current moment.

A beautiful, healthy, happy and peaceful women who is leaving out her dreams and creating new ones daily.

So hear me when I say that I am not telling you anything that I heard, I am not telling you a theory.

I am telling you what I KNOW works.

I am telling you the tales of women that is WHOLE but was once damaged.

I am telling you this so that you too can stop being broken and damaged by the will of yourself.

I'll share this secret, it's no one else's responsibility but your OWN.

As we travel our journeys we will still remain human, we will still fall short at times.

There will be times when doing what is best for you won't always align with what is best for everyone else around you and that is okay.

As long as you are operating from a place with great integrity and honor you will have the ability to make sound and wise decisions that will have lasting impact on your character and your greater you.

Not everyone will understand and you have to be okay with that. Those people who love you anyways are the people who deserve the version of you that you are seeking.

## Number 2: Love on YOURSELF

Self-Love is a word that is often thrown around a lot without a true sense of what it means. It's easy to say I love myself but does the way you treat yourself reflect the true action of love. Truly being in love with you takes for you to have a deeper sense of who you are as a person.

By definition *Self-love is a state of appreciation for oneself that grows from actions that support our physical, psychological and spiritual growth. Self-love means having a high regard for your own well-being and happiness. Self-love means taking care of your own needs and not sacrificing your well-being to please others.*

It both empowers us to take risks and to say no to things that don't work for us. It's a key component of building self-compassion. Self-love helps us take care of ourselves, lower stress, and strive for success.

At the core of self-love lies embracing your uniqueness. Each one of us possesses a distinct set of qualities, strengths, and talents that shape our identity. Acknowledging and appreciating these traits is the initial step towards self-love.

HERE ARE 8 IMPORTANT STEPS TO EMBRACING YOUR UNIQUENESS:

1. Accept who you are. It's difficult to be different if you refuse to accept your identity.

2. Everyone has a story to tell, listen to them and find your own.

3. Stop trying to compromise on who you are.

4. Find your crowd and people with similar interests.

5. Embrace your talents and skills and accept them for what they are.

6. Embrace your beliefs and don't change them to fit other's views.

7. Spend time doing what you love and not just what you have to do.

8. Accept criticism and encompass it into your life.

Embracing your individual uniqueness will release a much stronger understanding and will allow you to speak highly to yourself about yourself you will begin to affirm: I'm *worthy! I'm exceptional and made for greatness! I'm significant just the way I am? My gifts and talents will change the world! I am a work of art? I accept myself even if I'm not perfect! Perfection is unattainable!*

Self-love can mean something different for each person because we all have many different ways to take care of ourselves. Figuring out what self-love looks like for you as an individual is an important part of your mental health and getting out of your own way.

### What does self-love mean to you?

For starters, it can mean:

- Talking to and about yourself with love
- Prioritizing yourself
- Giving yourself a break from self-judgement
- Trusting yourself
- Being true to yourself
- Being nice to yourself
- Setting healthy boundaries
- Forgiving yourself when you aren't being true or nice to yourself

For many people, self-love is another way to say self-care. To exercise self-care, we often need to go back to the fundamentals and

- Listen to our bodies

- Take breaks from work and move/stretch.

- Put the phone down and connect to yourself or others, or do something creative like writing, painting, etc.

- Eating healthily, but sometimes indulge in your favorite foods.

Self-love means accepting yourself as you are in this very moment for everything that you are. It means accepting your emotions for what they are and putting your physical, emotional and mental well-being first.

### How and Why to Practice Self Love

So now we know that self-love motivates you to make healthy choices in life. When you hold yourself in high esteem, you're more likely to choose things that nurture your well-being and serve you well.

Ways to practice self-love include:

- **Becoming mindful.** People who have more self-love tend to know what they think, feel, and want.

- **Taking actions based on need rather than want.** By staying focused on what you need, you turn away from automatic behavior patterns that get you into trouble, keep you stuck in the past, and lessen self-love.

- **Practicing good self-care.** You will love yourself more when you take better care of your basic needs. People high in self-love nourish themselves daily through healthy activities, like sound nutrition, exercise, proper sleep, intimacy and healthy social interactions.

- **Making room for healthy habits.** Start truly caring for yourself by mirroring that in what you eat, how you exercise, and what you spend time doing. Do stuff, not to "get it done" or because you "have to," but because you care about you.

Finally, to practice self-love, start by being kind, patient, gentle and compassionate to yourself, the way you would with someone else that you care about.

These things were instrumental in my personal journey to loving me, understanding me and surviving me.

Let's drive a bit further into our thoughts. As I said above transforming your mind can transform your life.

I had to condition my mind. Everything in life is mental. Once you master your thoughts you are headed sown the right path.

I have a saying that if you can't control your thoughts, you can't control your words and if you can't control your words, you can't control your actions.

This is a dangerous place and will only contribute to you standing right smack in the center of your demise.

Your thoughts have the power to stop you from taking action towards moving forward in your journey.

Mastering your mind helps to achieve your long-term goals, reduces worries and anxiety, equips you against unhealthy habits, leads to better physical health, better relationships and gives you more resilience and more happiness.

Self-awareness is the starting place to control your thoughts.

You need to become aware of the thoughts as they come. Observing your thoughts and reflecting upon them is how you gain this skill. It's most important to identify your negative thoughts so that you can unpack them and get to a source of where they stem from.

I would classify negative thoughts as those that are the most harmful to us. It's these kinds of thoughts that reduce the quality of our relationships and makes us procrastinate.

Here are some of the most destructive ones:

- Blaming: both yourself, other people, or outside circumstances

- Comparing: yourself to your previous self or others

- Polarizing: e.g. if I don't win now, then I can't ever win anything

- Mind reading: thinking that you know exactly what others think of you

Once you've identified a negative thought, it's time to reveal the pattern. This means understanding what triggers the thought. To understand what happens to you when the thought appears. And how you behave as a result of it.

Do these thoughts occur when you're in a specific place? Or perhaps when you're around a specific group of people? Or maybe it's a specific situation?

Once you figure out when the thought occurs most often, look at the rest of the pattern. Observe how you feel once that thought crosses your mind. How do your feelings then influence your thinking? How does your physical body react? And how do you behave as a result of it?

When you experience the negative thought, you now have the choice: to interrupt or to let it run the show.

Instead of letting it run the show, choose to interfere.

Ask yourself why you should believe your thoughts. Why is it true? Or where is this coming from?

Question your negative thoughts enough and you will break the automatic loop of them just running wild in your life.

Being in control of your thoughts brings you many different benefits that touch every aspect of your life. Our human brain works hard, both professionally and personally, so the benefits of controlling your mind stretch far and wide.

Here are several benefits you can experience from controlling your mind:

- You know how to set boundaries in your relationships because you know what you want and need

- Your thoughts are more purposeful and meaningful

- You can develop healthier well-being in life

- You can overcome any challenges you face in a constructive, effective way

- You have more insight when it comes to making decisions

- You have a greater sense of self-awareness

- You sleep better at night because your mind is calm

Having control over our minds helps us to achieve our short-term and long-term goals. It helps us get through our days professionally and personally with a clear, confident, growth mindset. It's hard to achieve our goals when our minds are under attack — especially when the attack comes from within ourselves.

These attacks can distract us, make us doubt ourselves, and derail our progress. But what you pay attention to affects your life. If you can learn to dismiss your negative thoughts, you'll have an easier time keeping a positive mindset.

Try to keep your attention on avoiding negative thinking. With a more focused mindset that isn't weighed down by unwanted thoughts, we can reach what we set out to achieve.

We've talked a lot about our thoughts, but we can't forget that we need to be aware of our body state and feelings to control our minds. Since our mind, body, and emotions are all connected, we have to think about our WHOLENESS

A WHOLENESS approach to living means that it's all about you. You're in the driver's seat detailing what emotions you feel, how your body is doing, and what's going on in your mind. And each part is just as important as the next. You can't disregard how your physical body feels when you're trying to learn how to control your subconscious mind and vice versa. Striving for a balance between our mind, body, and soul will help us achieve a healthy overall well-being.

You can't change your life if you're neglecting one area because it seems unimportant. You're a WHOLE Person, and you need to take care of your WHOLE Self.

It's important to remind yourself that you're in control. Nobody else will best tell you what thoughts you should or shouldn't be thinking, so it's up to you to put in the work. Sometimes it can be intimidating to challenge your unwanted thoughts and do the necessary hard work to expel them. But being brave and dealing with the negative thoughts now will make room for healthier, more positive thinking in the future.

Ask yourself: *Will you let your mind control you, or will you work toward learning how to control your mind?*

It won't happen with the snap of your fingers, but with sustained effort, you'll be able to focus your thoughts on more productive, positive things.

Here are some healthy tips to help you learn how to control your mind:

- Practice mindfulness meditation and breathing exercises

- Include positive affirmations in your self-talk rather than put-downs

- Take a pause during your day to slow your mind down

- Avoid things that trigger negative thoughts, like scrolling through social media

- Ask self-evaluating questions if you're confused or unsure how to think

- Work on challenging your inner critic and changing your perspective on situations to be more positive

- Journal down your thoughts to let them out and express your feelings

- Talk with a therapist, life coach, or a trusted friend and loved one for support

- Learn that it's OK to acknowledge your thoughts, but let go of the ones that don't serve your purpose

- Stop listening to negative, pessimistic people and the advice they give you

- Practice positive visualization when you become overwhelmed with unwanted thoughts

- Distract yourself — whether that's calling a friend, watching a show, or going for a walk

# CHAPTER TWO:

## IT'S OKAY TO HEAL!

*"The thief comes only to steal and kill and destroy; I came that they may have life and have it abundantly" (John 10:10).*

What would it be like to walk away from a yearly review knowing confidently who you are in Christ despite what your boss said?

To put aside social media, and find joy in your present season of life? To silence the voice inside your head that says, "You are a failure" and instead, hear the words that "You are enough" or "You are worthy".

We've all heard the term "time heals all wounds", if this is so why then when your boss tells you that your work is inadequate, do you hear the faint whisper of a parent telling you your grades aren't good enough? Or when you scroll through Instagram, do you feel that same chill of imperfection as you did at 15, navigating high school for the first time.

I know this saying has probably been used by most of your notable motivational speakers, public figures and elders well unfortunately I must disrupt this thought.

"Time does not heal all wounds".

I would say vulnerability, bravery, and a desire to change does.

Pain isn't our enemy. Pain isn't the problem. The problem is our unwillingness to validate our pain or fear to face it.

Let us see our pain as a deeper call towards healing. Whether you want to work through major traumatic life events or have a desire to address the daily causes of anxiety, fear, and negative self-talk. There is hope for our chains to be broken from our past wounds.
Not by giving time, but by allowing yourself a place to process and piece together truth. It is here that you find freedom from the past.

Healing happens when you're willing to see how you're trapped, and you do whatever it takes to be free.

Please allow me to add that healing from my past pain and trauma has been the most liberating thing I have been able to accomplish in this life. It has been the mere center of all of my success and I know that it will continue to be the gateway to my bright future.

Let's go look into the choices necessary get to our healing.

You've probably been gripped by your reactions to past events for a long time. So it will take your focus and pure intention to engage in this process of healing.

**GET FED UP,** Be thoroughly sick of the emotional agony, the riff in your relationships, and the half-life you are living. Vow to see your way to freedom.

**GIVE UP THE VICTIM,** This mindset does not serve your happiness. Replace it with openness, inquisitiveness, and the readiness to see things in a new and fresh way. Take full responsibility for your happiness.

**GIVE UP OLD IDENTITY,** identity is a fixed idea that you think describes who you are. If you've been living in the pain from your past, you might see yourself as wounded, needy, lacking, or broken. All of these identities limit you from seeing your natural brilliance. It's like you're looking at yourself through a window with broken glass. See yourself as you actually are, not how your conclusions from your past experiences tell you are.

**BE REALISTIC,** Healing from the pain of the past doesn't mean your memories are erased or that you'll never have those difficult feelings again. However, it does mean that when these experiences come, they don't get to be in charge. They stop defining you. They no longer direct your actions. When a memory or emotion appears – and it will, don't touch it. Don't feed it with your attention, and it will go just as fast as it came. This is real, effortless freedom. Any experience can arise, but you remain stable, undisturbed, and FREE.

**FORGIVENESS,** Forgiveness of others may happen, but for now you need to focus on yourself. Discover in every moment how attachment to thoughts and feelings makes you unhappy. Then let these go for your own well-being. Some of your thoughts may have to do with regret about your own actions. Wherever you are stuck, keep at it to find your way to peace.

**ELIMINATE BELIEFS THAT KEEP YOU STUCK**, if the
process of healing hits a roadblock, you may hold some
hidden beliefs that are controlling your happiness.
Consider these:

- I feel justified in staying upset because I was
  wronged.
- If I let go, I'm approving others' bad behavior.
- I need an apology.

These beliefs have only one purpose – **to keep you a
victim of your past.**

**LET THE PAST BE THE PAST,** the past is gone. And if
it's still a problem, that problem is happening now, in
this present moment and you need to further address
this.

You can't rewrite the past, but you can absolutely learn
to relate to it differently so that you're no longer
triggered. Live only according to what's true, and let the
rest go. Put aside any self-imposed limits. You'll be
amazed by the potential for happiness and fulfillment
that's been here all along – once you're free from the pain
of your past.

Subconsciously we carry the past, into the present moment and spoil the present moments. We automatically do that. We're programmed to do that. We'd rather live in our virtual reality of what happened to me in the past and what should've happened and what could've happened and what would've happened if somebody didn't do this or that. We'd rather live in the story about how my life is going and what I want and what my life will be like in the future than just be in life as it is right now.

*Growth demands a temporary surrender of security.*

*– Gail Sheehy*

However, pain is real, it deserves validation and recognition. We cannot go throughout our whole life just acting as if they never happened or never addressing them.

It took me a long time to understand this concept with some of my own childhood trauma. I believed that if I just learned to move forward that I would be okay. It was when I desired to elevate higher that I concluded some issues needed to be verbally expressed.

I have always been a great writer and it is one of my forms of self-care but there is a huge healing difference in written and oral.

It is often most painful to say things aloud, because they tap into a vulnerability that we often like to hide.

It was terrifying for me to speak about how things had hurt me and how because of my hurt I had learned to protect myself from everything and everyone.

I covered my pain in dishonesty. I had to dig deep to understand that this not only affected me but the ones that I loved. I felt justified because I had not dealt with my own pain.
Once I let go of my justification, spoke my truth aloud and forgave myself I instantly became FREE.

Of course the work did not just stop there but that provided this huge sense of relief. I had a longing to just be WHOLE, to just be HAPPY and to just be FREE.

I had no desire to be hurt or to be bound. I just wanted to LIVE and live abundantly.

This desire came with many sacrifices. You have to be willing to give up things to make room for new things.

To be happy, there is one thing you have to surrender — YOU. You have to surrender YOU in order to be happy, in order to be awaken, and in order to love. And since the YOU is created by thoughts about the past and thoughts about the present and thoughts about the future, you have to be willing to surrender those thoughts.

We must also learn the value in forgiveness.

Forgiveness gets us beyond the past. We forgive for ourselves. We do it for ourselves, to free us from the suffering caused by our thoughts about the past. Forgiveness is emotional hygiene—because if you carry the past into the present moment, you'll be unhappy, it will limit you, it will keep you involved with the ego and all of its misperceptions, desires, and lies.

What we're really doing when we forgive is we're just letting everything be as it is and letting everything be as it was—realizing that we can't change what happened in the past, knowing in our hearts that we've learned from all of it, and in that sense, whatever happened in the past was the right experience.

Life is a school. The only way we grow and evolve is by making mistakes. That's how we find out what works and what doesn't work. There is no manual that tells us how to go about life without making mistakes. The manual is the mistake. The mistake is the manual.

Move past the mistakes, past the hurt and unlock a new chapter.

# CHAPTER THREE:

## PEACE IS EXPENSIVE

*PEACE – (noun) freedom from disturbance; tranquility.*

Peace means societal friendship and harmony in the absence of hostility and violence. In a social sense, peace is commonly used to mean a lack of conflict and freedom from fear. "Psychological peace" (such as peaceful thinking and emotions) is less well-defined, yet perhaps a necessary predecessor to establishing "behavioral peace".

Peaceful behavior sometimes results from a "peaceful inner disposition". It has been argued by some that inner qualities such as tranquility, patience, respect, compassion, kindness, self-control, courage, moderation, forgiveness, equanimity, and the ability to see the big picture can promote peace within an individual, regardless of the external circumstances of their life.

Most people desire peace, and understand how peace is a key to happiness. Peace is for me the most beautiful thing on this Earth it allows for a harmony within that is priceless. What I don't think we talk about enough is how expensive PEACE really is.

Peace is no cheap date. It comes with a HUGE price tag, it costs more than the most expensive designer you have in your closet but has more value than any material possessions.

It will cost you discomfort and growing pains. To acquire this intangible thing you must often be willing to sacrifice people, places and things. You sometimes even have to give up physical and financial stability because you are choosing PEACE.

What happens when the very things that cost you your peace are the same exact things that you love and cherish such as your family or friends, sometimes even your adult children or spouse? That is a very difficult place to be in and it's often that we struggle with choosing US. We have become so dedicated to who and what we are for other people that we neglect ourselves in the process.

Choosing peace looks different for everyone. Sometimes you do have to do a complete sever from people but often you can just set boundaries. You will know what that looks like for each situation. The key here again is being honest with who disrupts your peace and not be so caught up on who they are but what matters is how they affect you.

Understand that boundaries are healthy, you can love and respect a person and still have boundaries with your access. It is also very important to categorize people in your life. Just because she is your sister does not mean that she is healthy for your mind. That also means that because you choose when and how you deal does not mean that you don't love her. That means that you love yourself and you realize that for you to be able to fully given anyone anything you are to be at a peaceful place within.

Stop apologizing for your inner peace, it does not have to up for discussion or compromise.

We you start to value peace you come in agreement that you must limit what you give your energy too. Because energy cannot be created or destroyed but simple transferred from one thing to another it is important that you surround yourself with people and places that give you peace.

Let's break down *PEACE*

*PEACE* stands for
Positive
Energy
Activates
Constant
Elevation.

We your surround yourself with positive energy it activates your ability to elevate in life in all areas.
If you focus your thoughts, words, and actions on creating more **positive energy**, your life will improve in ways you now believe impossible. Everything in your life and everyone in your path will move to a **higher plane** of vibration.

Positive people are a source of inspiration and motivation. They can help you stay focused on your goals and overcome challenges. They offer constructive criticism and feedback, helping you grow and improve. Positive people also have a contagious energy that can uplift your spirits and boost your confidence.

On the other hand, negative people can bring you down and drain your energy.

The only path to peace — to move out what is disturbing the peace.

Nevertheless, there will come a time when you will want peace more than you want drama, and peace will be there, waiting for you, in the silence, where it has always been.

# CHAPTER FOUR:

## FAITH OVER FEAR

Fear is a natural response to challenges or the unknown. Fear is the biggest reason why people don't do what they love or go toward what they are interested in. Some fear is healthy, such as the kind we need for our survival and protection.

The kind of fear that holds us back, though, is irrational fear – the stories we make up in our mind that aren't based in reality.

Judgment is another reason, either one's own judgments or other people's judgments. If, for instance, you grew up around people who didn't value art, then you might have taken on their judgments about it and stopped yourself from even considering pursuing art as a hobby or more serious pursuit.

Without your fears or judgments, what do you want to spend your time doing? What are you interested in? What do you enjoy? What excites you? What do you want to learn more about or get better at? The answers to these questions are clues to your life purpose. All you have to do is let yourself be free to do what you are moved to do without prejudging that or stopping yourself from doing that for any other reason.

Now you're out of your own way, and unchained from your past. No longer needing to figure it all out, you're available to the natural unfolding of the flow of life. Transform yourselves in order to transform the world. There is only hope if enough people choose to align with the truth of their being, with peace and love. There is only hope if you make a choice to stand with the truth and live the truth.

Don't let others determine what your life is about. This is for you to determine. You are the one living your life, and you are the one who must live with the consequences of your choices. This is your life, and it is a unique life. It will not be like anyone else's life who has ever or will ever live.

Fear leads to procrastination and that makes it more difficult to take charge of your life, achieve your goals and have a well-ordered existence filled with happiness and satisfaction.

You can move through that fear. You can use it to push past your comfort zone, and to grow in the process. Once you realize how much fear has unnecessarily held you back, and begin to experience "wins" as a result of pushing through those fears, you can use that momentum to fuel success – however you define it. When it comes to pursuing your purpose, you really can't afford to sit around second guessing yourself. If you give fear an inch it will take a mile. Trust God and go ALL IN.

Here are six (6) ways to overcome fear, and create the success you desire:

## 1. Put it in Perspective
As I wrote earlier, some fear is healthy, while other fear holds us back. Understanding the difference between the two will help you to put your fear in its proper perspective when it shows up. Ideally, you will get to a place where you can treat your apprehension as information, rather than as a barrier.

## 2. Name It
What is it that you fear? What's standing in the way of accomplishing your goals and aspirations? Invest some time identifying what's holding you back. Acknowledge it, and think about where those feelings are coming from.

## 3. Confront It
"Do the thing you fear and the death of fear is certain." This quote encourages us to face our fears head on. When you do the very thing you fear, you often discover your anxiety was just an illusion – a story you made up in your mind.

## 4. Do something Bold
It doesn't eliminate the fear, but rather shows us how to take action in spite of that fear.
Like when you get on the airplane for this first time doing something bold is empowering, to say the least. With your bold experience, you'll be reminded that you can do *anything* you put your mind to.

## 5. Be willing to FAIL

In the pursuit of a goal, especially one of great significance, it's rare that we accomplish it without struggle. There are obstacles in our path, and navigating through them, or around them, or over them, is part of the process.

Most people hate failure, so they avoid taking action that might cause them to fail. Instead of avoiding what you fear, what if you treated failure as a stepping stone to success?

Those who have achieved significant success have done so because of their willingness to fail. Instead of thinking of failure as the enemy of success, they use failure as an opportunity to learn. They're not intimidated by failure – we embrace it as part of the process.

## 6. Seek Support

Risk is scary, and sometimes you need a little help to navigate through the uncertainty, and achieve your goals. Whether you work with a coach, or simply talk with a friend or accountability partner, objective feedback from others can provide another perspective, and help you see things you might not notice on your own.

Fear is an emotion that can be overcome with practice. In time, it will no longer hold you back, regardless of the outcome. You'll develop the resilience needed to persevere through temporary adversity, and to redefine failure as learning lessons that move you closer to your goals. Your approach to goal achievement will be strengthened, and you will come to realize that you are stronger than any obstacle standing in your way.

To fully know what we are capable of doing, we can't let our fears hold us back.

I hope that, whatever it is you're facing, whatever fears you have, you can also learn to push through them and grow from them.

Is fear holding you back from your full potential? What things might God be calling you to do right now that you will just have to do scared in order to follow Him? If you're scared, know that you are not alone, and don't let your fears keep you from fully living and doing all that God calls us to do.

I am a women of faith and that faith carries me through. Along with better mental habits I also know that I must look within God's word for confirmation.

1. *"Fear not, for I am with you; be not dismayed, for I am your God. I will strengthen you, I will help you, I will uphold you with my righteous right hand."* **Isaiah 41:10**

2. *"Be strong and courageous. Do not fear or be in dread of them, for it is the LORD your God who goes with you. He will not leave you or forsake you."* **Deuteronomy 31:6**

3. *"Peace I leave with you; my peace I give to you. Not as the world gives do I give to you. Let not your hearts be troubled, neither let them be afraid."* **John 14:27**

The truth of God's Word and His promises bridge the gap between the fear you feel and what you know to be true about God and His love for you. Renewing your mind through the memorization of His Word is the best defense against the fears of this world.

# CHAPTER FIVE:

## GOOD FRIENDS MATTER

"Make friends" isn't just something we tell our kids to do on the first day of school — positive friendships are important for adults, too. Now might be a good time to think about friendships that are especially meaningful to you. I've found that as people talk about their friends, they are often talking about their current self or the self they'd like to become.

People need people. It's one of those basic truths of life. We all need friends to help us when we're down and friends to laugh with us when we're up. But all friendships are not created equal. Some are worth investing more into, while others can drag us down.

Along those same lines, if you realize that a particular relationship doesn't reflect your values, it's okay to say goodbye. We are often afraid to let go of friendships — maybe for the nostalgia of the past, the thought that they may be useful in the future, or how it looks to others when we have fewer friends. However, there are times when it is not just okay but helpful for our success and self-identity to let a friendship fade away or break away.

Sometimes you must analyze if you are the one bringing negative things into the friendships. So what makes a good friend, anyways? And what makes a bad one? There's a lot of opinions and advice out there, but these quotes I've been proven true in my life over and over again.

**Good Friends Give Honest Advice**
"The sweetness of a friend comes from their honest advice."

**We Become the People We Surround Ourselves With**
"Walk with the wise and become wise, for a companion of fools suffers harm."

**Good Friends Stick Around. Bad Ones Run Away.**
"One who has unreliable friends soon comes to ruin, but there is a friend who sticks closer than a brother/sister."

A good friend shows up no matter what. A true friend supports and encourages us, tolerates our shortcomings, accepts us unconditionally, and cares for us no matter what.

True friends walk through life together. A real friend bears witness to whatever happens to you. A true friend shares our joys and sorrows. Friends can be family. Sometimes our friends are the family we wished we had.

A friend rekindles our light when it has gone out, ignites our excitement, and inspires us to do better and more. A real friend may even inspire you in a way you never imagined you could be. They may wake you up to all of the possibilities that lives within you and help you to realize your full potential.

But friends do a lot more than give you a shoulder to cry on; they also have a positive impact on your health. Some research even says friendships are just as important to your well-being as eating right and exercising
When you are on this journey of surviving you, you should take inventory of your friends and realize how much your friends may be a reflection of where you are in life. Quality counts more than quantity. While it may be good to cultivate a diverse network of friends and acquaintances, you may feel a greater sense of belonging and well-being by nurturing close, meaningful relationships that will support you through thick and thin

You can assess your friends by asking yourself: Do my friends:
- Increase my sense of belonging and purpose
- Boost my happiness and reduce my stress
- Improve my self-confidence and self-worth
- Help me cope with traumas, such as divorce, serious illness, job loss or the death of a loved one
- Encourage me to change or avoid unhealthy lifestyle habits, such as excessive drinking or lack of exercise

Developing and maintaining healthy friendships involves give-and-take. Sometimes you're the one giving support, and other times you're on the receiving end. Letting friends know you care about them and appreciate them can help strengthen your bond. It's as important for **you to be a good friend** as it is to surround yourself with good friends.

Foster ways to be a good steward of your friends:

**Be kind.** This most-basic behavior remains the core of successful relationships.

**Be a good listener**. Ask what's going on in your friends' lives. When friends share details of hard times or difficult experiences, be empathetic, but don't give advice unless your friends ask for it.

**Open up.** Build intimacy with your friends by opening up about yourself. Being willing to disclose personal experiences and concerns shows that your friend holds a special place in your life, and it may deepen your connection.

**Show that you can be trusted.** Being responsible, reliable and dependable is key to forming strong friendships. When your friends share confidential information, keep it private.

As we strive to improve, we don't do it alone when we have good friends. Our true friends help us on this journey. They are there to support and listen, but they are also not afraid to say the hard thing.

Real friends will tell you if you need to have a better relationship with someone, if the person you are dating is unhealthy for you, or if it is time to find a new job. These friends will tell you what you need to hear not what you want to hear but they have an understanding that the manner in which this is done is just as important.

Value good friends don't take them for granted and don't allow yourself to be taken for granted. This all goes hand in hand.

# CHAPTER SIX:

## HAPPINESS IS A CHOICE

### LIFE IS ABOUT CHOICES.
*Life is a matter of choices, and every choice you make, makes you. – John C. Maxwell.*

Life is made up of an infinite amount of choices. Most decisions, are small and only slightly impactful, but it's the big decisions, the ones that can change your life forever, that are tough to make.

Most of our days are filled with choices, big and small, and they all matter, even when we aren't making any. Are we where we want to be? Are we happy, sad or indifferent? Wherever we find ourselves is a direct result of the choices we have made up to this point in life.

Some choices might have seemed inconsequential, while others were major life choices. In the end, all of these choices form together to create the person we are today and the life we live. The choices we make today will impact our lives tomorrow.

I believe we can make good choices when we weigh up the consequences and the possibilities, and stay true to our morals and values and ensure that fears and doubts aren't impacting our decisions. Sometimes, it's got to do with family background or parental influence. Or educational and academic experiences that determine our ability to make choices soundly.

But seriously, what are some of the most important factors in determining the outcome of our lives?

In spite of the importance of this question, many of us don't give much serious thought to the answer. We just go with the flow and let our lives work out in their own way. Granted, it's much easier to just let life happen and not be personally responsible for the actual results. However, life doesn't just happen. Instead, our lives are defined by the choices we make.

One of the great things about having the power to choose is that if you don't like the place you are in your life right now, you can change it! You're in the driver's seat, and you can actively and intentionally pursue different options for yourself. It's part of your decision-making on how to be happy in life.

## IT'S YOUR RIGHT TO CHOOSE HAPPINESS!

Is happiness a choice? Yes, but it requires more than just saying *"I choose to be happy"*. Sustaining happiness in your life takes commitment, courage, and a deep understanding of who you are and who you're becoming. By choosing to embrace happiness in your life, you're taking on the responsibility of your own contentment.

If you want positive things to happen for you in life, then you must choose daily to sow positivity into your Life. Plant seeds of positive thinking and positive action every day, and before long, you will have a fantastic garden of very positive and amazing things happening FOR you in life.

*By choosing to focus daily on positivity, you will quickly be surprised at how much you're able to achieve and how much happier you're becoming.*

Positive affirmations spoken daily and aloud are very powerful because they take charge of your thoughts. The sound of your voice has a tremendous influence over your subconscious, and more than any other voice.

*You can literally speak happiness into your Life.*

Choose to start the day on your terms. People who know how to use their mornings get more done by noon than most do all week. *How we start our day determines how we create our Life. Are you sleeping through your morning…snoozing through your Life…and snoozing through your unlimited potential?*

Starting your day early creates confidence, and when we're confident, we're happy.

Happiness does not demand some external event, an accomplishment, a win, a pat on the head, a struggle or any reason at all.

Be Grateful
*"When I started counting my blessings, my whole life turned around." — Willie Nelson*

Maintaining a sense of gratitude and everyday happiness can easily slip off your to do list, especially when life is busy and sometimes down right tough. For me, I have a teenager, two small children, I work a full time career, I am the founder of a nonprofit, I run my boutique businesses from home and in the last few years my spouse and I have both lost family members including him losing a parent something that I have already experienced.

We have had to face the usual pile of low level crap that life has to offer. From mortgages, bills, family dramas and the general stress of being a responsible adult. So in short, I completely get it that life can sometimes seem to do it's best to keep happiness at bay.

It's easy to see happiness as an ideal that's kept at arm's length – a beautiful fantasy that 'one day' you'll be able to have access too – if only you can wade through all the day-to-day crap first. But it doesn't have to be that way. By switching your thinking to consciously choose happy, every single day, you'll soon start to see the positives that are all around you.

While embracing my happiness I leaned more into a few things to help me along the way. Happiness for me had a ton to do with my spiritual journey with Christ.

I have always believed that when the Lord shows you something or bring something to your attention through the Holy Spirit, he then enables you to go forth, so I was really excited about what he had shown me. Believing and hoping that God would reward my obedience to his Word and change my heart and perspective so that I could live out, what he had shown me.

*My motivation was obedience.*

For me it was very intentional that I was obedient to the word of God and understanding the course of my happiness and my strength to be happy. Then the Lord showed me the power of renewing your mind. I was experiencing life, the fruit of my obedience, and the intimacy with God that was so beautiful.

Joy comes when we totally surrender to God and live life led by the Holy Spirit.

I am praying for you on your pursuit, that you would find JOY, real joy. I pray that the Holy Spirit would make himself very real to you, thru your circumstances. Deeper places, deeper connection.
That your eyes and ears would be opened to Him and the beautiful plan He has for your life, that as you wrap yourself up in Him, you would fall in love with the one who is greater than life itself and you will then choose HAPPINESS.

If you take anything from this chapter take these small nuggets to unlock your own happiness.

## Design your days

People who feel unhappy are often time poor and feel out of control with how they spend their time. So make sure you stay in charge. Get boundaries around your time.

## Say NO with a smile

Learn to say no. When you learn to say no you can walk away from a situation owning your power and feeling positive that you respect yourself, your limits and your time. No is a complete sentence.

## Find those silver linings

If something irritating happens during your day, it's about trying to find the silver lining. Life is always throwing unexpected things in our paths, so choosing to find the positive is a worthy skill to practice. Your thoughts and how you react to things is so powerful.

## Prioritize yourself

I know first-hand how difficult it is to make yourself important when you have hundreds of other priorities and people competing for your time and energy. However, choosing happiness means choosing yourself in some small way, every single day.

# CHAPTER SEVEN:

# IT ALL WORKS TOGETHER FOR THE GOOD

*And we know that all things work together for good to them that love God, to them who are the called according to his purpose.*
*Romans 8:28*

I recall going through a really heavy storm in my life. The storm was so bad, I often wondered when it would just be over. I was tired, I began to feel defeated. I just wanted to know why me?
Why would I have to continue to go through the valleys of life? My mind was clouded with worry, fear and confusion.

This when Chapter 5 really played out in my life. I have been tremendously blessed with wonder friends, one who pray for me, inspire me and lift me up.

I understood that being vulnerable with my circle would help me to navigate these lows, I did not need to be alone in my mind with all my thoughts. It was imperative that I had a sounding board. Multiple sounding boards to be exact but my friends all served individual purposes I did not go to them all for the same advice. I have my praying friends, I have my fun friends and I have my highly successful friends.

Having this outlet helped me to sort out thing that I already knew and to allow me to gain new outlook in many areas. My circle is FREEING, it's safe and it's full of wisdom.

It was not only my circle but my desire to walk in all my fullness. I knew that the Bible talked about all things working together for the greater good.

If we are not careful, we might think that Romans 8:28 is telling us that things work together for our good on their own. However, in light of the biblical teaching on divine providence, as well as the immediate context, Paul is really telling us that God Himself is the One who works all things together for our good. He works out all things according to the counsel of His will. God's purpose in creating and redeeming us is to reveal and magnify His glory. In working all things together for good, God is simultaneously working all things together for His glory.

Romans 8:28 does not guarantee a trouble-free life or justify suffering but rather highlights that God works all things together for the good of those who love Him and are called according to His purpose.

This verse calls us to reorient ourselves and change our perspective regarding our circumstances.

It teaches that God is at work in every aspect of our lives, and we should align ourselves with His purpose to experience His blessings and development.

Romans 8:28 is a conditional promise for those who love God and are called according to His purpose.

Our love for God is demonstrated through obedience to His word, and aligning our lives with His purpose allows us to experience the fullness of this promise.

The promise of Romans 8:28, while it does not guarantee a painless life, assures us that God can use our suffering for our ultimate good and the good of others.

Let the story unfold. Sometimes a bad event happens and good things come out of it as a result. Other times, good things happen and bad things happen as a result. The reality is good and bad events flow in and out of each other.

Joy and Pain are one in the same, and it's also okay to find joy in a simple moment or create a meaningful moment in the midst of chaos, uncertainty, fear, and even grief. You see, joy and pain can actually peacefully co-exist. If we keep our eyes and heart open to that possibility, we may find purpose and connection in these experiences.

I reference the unexpected death of my father a lot because this may be the most significant and impactful moment of my entire life in both a positive and negative way.

Of course hind sight is always 20-20 and I didn't always feel the way I now do 18 years later however life has revealed itself as I have matured over the years from child to adult. I spent many years fantasizing about how my life would have played out if my dad had never passed.

Now I wonder if I would be as resilient as I am now, if he were still living. I have learned to understand that I cannot go back and undo what God saw fit for my life and rather allowing myself to sit in pain and I found solace in changing the way I thought about my grief. Please understand that this has been a very long process, this thinking did not just appear overnight. It took many years of working through all the emotions and triggers that were attached to losing my dad.

Greif is a whole different matter that we could write an entire book on attempting to unpack but for the purpose of this subject matter I want the topic to circle back to joy and pain intertwining and that being acceptable.

I now understand that life ebbs and flows, it peaks and valleys and there will be sunshine and rain.
All these things hold value to our overall existence. Too much of either can be unhealthy and we cannot try and avoid the bad days. It's in the bad days that we learn the most.

Nature constantly reminds us that sometimes it takes a breakdown to have a major breakthrough.
Pain has a powerful way of teaching us what's most important and where our true purpose lies.

My character was revealed the most in my lowest moments, I learned a lot about who a really was.

The best thing you can do in these moments is sit there for a moment, hear me. I did NOT SAY stay there I said sit there for a brief moment and understand what lesson you should take away that will help you in the next phase of your life.

See these lessons are the keys to unlock doors of the opportunities that are ahead.

Some of the most precious things in life are birthed from adversity. Caterpillars becoming butterflies. Babies being born is the most traumatic and beautiful thing. The world around us is jam-packed with incredible miracles every day.

While there is tremendous pain, suffering and uncertainty all around us, there also is an opportunity for change. Because when things go wrong, there is also a greater opportunity to turn things around for the better. Our difficult seasons can also be a chance for us to change directions and let go of what no longer serves us.

Trauma transforms us into different versions of ourselves. Whether those changes are for better or worse is largely up to the choices we make, our perception and overall mindset. Just because something happened; doesn't mean it will always be that way.

Everything changes once you can look back on the most difficult period in your life and feel gratitude instead of bitterness because you finally understand it was all part of a bigger plan. We eventually start to realize as difficult as that time was, it was really a catalyst pushing us further along towards realizing our life's purpose. When we are able to turn our pain into purpose, we start to melt away anger and resentment and replace it with joy and a renewed love of life.

Again for me, I did a ton of writing on my journey, it was a part of my therapy process.

I want to challenge you to do the same. I have created some additional writing space at the end of this book and I encourage you to take some time to reflect on the painful event.

Write down as many memories as you can recall from that time. Write whatever comes to mind. Don't worry about the order. Later you can go back and arrange the events chronologically. Also, don't worry about writing in full sentences or whether or not your grammar is correct. Let the contents of your mind and heart fill the pages without judgment or fear. Getting your thoughts on paper helps you make sense of how you are feeling. Once you are able to reflect on what you wrote down, you may start to notice some repeating themes or patterns. Learning how to observe how you are feeling about a particular event without judgement, guilt or shame is one of the first steps towards surviving.

Even now I have many notebooks and journals from my past and I often go back to and reflect on just how far I have come on my journey. It is refreshing to see the way my thoughts have evolved and to know that I am not repeating cycles to keep me stuck in one place.

I was driving down the street one day and I see a billboard that read:

*"Life can be both beautiful and difficult at the same time."*

This statement hit home for me because during that time I was experiencing fullness in my life yet I did not have all the things I wanted. Life was beautiful at the very same time I had some I was experiencing some difficulties however I had an extremely level of gratitude for where I was in this current moment, how far I had come from who I used to be and hopeful for things that I had not yet achieved.

Life was in fact beautiful and difficult at the same time.

# CHAPTER EIGHT:

## STAY ON YOUR P'S

*Prayer, Priorities, Peace & Positivity!*

These four word keep my grounded they are like and anchor to any situation, good or bad that I find myself in.

### PRAYER

*PRAYER an act of communication by humans with the sacred or holy — God, the gods, the transcendent realm, or supernatural powers. Found in all religions in all times, prayer may be a corporate or personal act utilizing various forms and techniques. Prayer has been described in its sublimity as "an intimate friendship, a frequent conversation held alone with God.*

Prayer is communicating with God. That can mean thanking Him, praising Him, confessing something you've done wrong or expressing a need you have. It can mean talking to Him as you would to a friend. Learning how to pray is really about developing a relationship with God. Relationships are built on moments of connection and communication. But how do you do that with the God of the universe?

Prayer is a supernatural activity. It's talking with a God who is unlike anyone else. He has a personality and qualities you can understand and relate to, but you cannot expect to relate to God in exactly the way you might to a close friend or family member. He's so much bigger and more incredible than that.

I was introduced to praying as a child, very simply we would kneel on the side of the bed at night and recite words that my grandma would speak, thanking God, asking for protection over ourselves and others and praying blessings over our home and others.

Of course being introduced to prayer at a young age helpd me to better understand that prayer is a source of building an intimate relationship with God.

It wasn't until I got a little older and my walk with God became strain to the point that I had "forgot" how to pray. But the Bible says "train a child and when they are older they will not depart."

This scripture let me know to know that simply closing my eyes and talking to God was all I needed to do to strengthen my prayer life again.

Those who never understood or were even taught to pray might ask things like:

**How Do You Pray?**
First, know that there is no secret formula to pray. God simply delights in us coming to Him in honesty.

You can start by addressing God directly in a way that acknowledges His uniqueness.

People will say things such as, "Father God," "Heavenly Father" or "Almighty God." How you choose to address Him will remind you of who you are talking to and what He represents in your life.

### When and where do I pray?
Anytime and anywhere can work, but it's helpful to find a distraction-free time and place if possible. God deserves your focused attention, and you might find it harder to listen to Him in a busy place.

Some people create a space in their homes, like a "prayer closet," for this purpose. Others will choose a favorite park or coffee shop.

### What position should I be in to pray?
You can bow, kneel, stand or walk around when you pray. God will hear you whatever you do, so choose a position that helps you focus.

Kneeling or bowing your head are great ways to focus your body and mind on God. It's a symbolic way to demonstrate that you respect His authority. John 17:1 also describes Jesus looking toward Heaven when praying.

**Do I pray to God the Father, Jesus or the Holy Spirit?**
This is completely up to you. Choose one or try praying
to each member of the Trinity at different times, because
they all listen to you. If you are a Christian, the Holy
Spirit is the presence of God living within you. So you
can address Him directly, with confidence that He is as
close as He could be.

Romans 8:26 says, "And the Holy Spirit helps us in our
weakness. For example, we don't know what God wants
us to pray for. But the Holy Spirit prays for us with
groanings that cannot be expressed in words"

**Should I pray out loud?**
Depending on your comfort level and situation, you can
choose whether to pray out loud or silently. Over time,
you will likely grow more comfortable praying out loud.

If you are praying for someone who is physically present
with you, it might encourage them to hear your faith
expressed through your prayers. But if you find praying
silently allows you to focus more on God, that's okay too.

Be sure to allow silence too so you can listen to God.
You'll find it harder to hear what He is saying if you are
doing all the talking.

**How do I end a prayer?**
A common way to end a prayer is by saying something
like, "In the name of Jesus, amen."
You don't need to close every prayer with a formal
ending for God to take you seriously.

## What Should You Pray For?

What's on your mind matters to God, because you matter to Him. As you develop the habit of praying, you will gain a sense of what God is talking to you about and what He thinks is worth your attention. In the beginning, try not to get too hung up on what you should be praying about. God has all the time in the world, and He's far more patient with us than we are with ourselves.

But if you're ever in doubt, pray like Jesus.

Jesus' closest friends asked Jesus to teach them how to pray. The result is the best-known prayer in human history — called the Lord's Prayer.

**Our Father in heaven, hallowed be Your name,
Your kingdom come, Your will be done, on earth as it is in heaven.
Give us today our daily bread.
And forgive us our debts, as we also have forgiven our debtors.
And lead us not into temptation, but deliver us from the evil one.**

**(Matthew 6:9-13, New International Version)**
Here are five lessons on prayer that we can learn from the example Jesus gives us in Matthew 6:9-13:
1. **"Our Father in heaven, hallowed be thy name."** Jesus starts by establishing our identity as children of God. He emphasizes this relationship as a source of confidence that God listens when you pray.

2. **"Your kingdom come, Your will be done, on earth as it is in heaven."**
It's tempting to rush to the part of prayer where you're asking God for what you want or need. But Jesus makes a point of placing God's agenda first. He also uses this phrase as a reminder that what is true of God in heaven is also true on earth.

3. **"Give us today our daily bread."**
Jesus models asking God for His own needs. Because God is a loving Father, He enjoys hearing what His children want and need, so that He can provide for them. Though He won't give you anything and everything you ask for, He will provide what you need to get through each day, including His grace to sustain you.

4. **"Forgive us our trust passing, as we forgive those who trust pass against us."**
Forgiveness was at the heart of Jesus' teaching during His time on earth, and it's here at the heart of His guide to prayer.
Jesus first models asking forgiveness for anything you have done that displeases God. Second, He reminds you to consider any unforgiveness you might have toward another person and ask Him to help you forgive them.

5. **"Lead us not into temptation, but deliver us from evil."**
Finally, Jesus closes His prayer by encouraging His followers to keep in mind that the Christian life is a spiritual battle with a very real enemy. Jesus closes His prayer by emphasizing how quickly and naturally humans stray from God's protection.

Reading the Lord's Prayer slowly and considering each idea is a great way to listen to God.

But this is just the beginning! The Bible suggests plenty of things that you can pray for at any time including:

- Your connection with God growing deeper day by day.
- Anything in your life getting in the way of your relationship with God.
- The people God wants you to express His love to.
- Your role as a representative for Jesus in the world (2 Corinthians 5:20).
- Your family, friends and career.
- How to manage the resources God has given you.
- Your understanding of the Bible.
- Developing the spiritual gifts the Holy Spirit has given to you.

Praying is not something that you can get wrong. It is the most valuable tool you can possess in life. You should pray with great expectation.

Every time you pray, you are saying, "In my own strength, I cannot do all that I want to do. I need help." Prayer is a way of inviting God into your life's struggles. Prayer can be a reminder that God is the source of strength, wisdom and inner peace.

Everyone is a control freak to one degree or another. Prayer allows you to admit to God that you need Him in the driver's seat of your life. As you continue to pray, you become more comfortable sharing your thoughts and feelings honestly with God. He knows everything about you and desires to hear from you the truth of how you are doing, both when things are good and when they are not.

If you are looking for ways to develop your prayer life I leave you with these two tips:

### 1. Pray in a Journal

*"Thoughts disentangle themselves when they pass through lips and fingertips." Dawson Trotman*

Writing out prayers and thoughts allows you to slow down and consider them more clearly. You could begin with a Bible verse that stands out to you, even if you don't know why it does.
Try asking yourself these simple questions as you read a Bible passage:

- What does this passage tell me about God?
- What feelings does this passage evoke in me and why?
- What thoughts or memories occur to me as I reflect on these verses?
- What could God want me to hear since this is what He gave me to read?

Answering these questions will help you reach a point where you can ask God how He wants you to respond to whatever you are reading.

God wants to speak to you, and He's not limited by how good a listener you are. So don't rush yourself, but trust the Holy Spirit, who lives inside you and helps you learn to recognize God's voice.

## 2. Pray With Other People

Listening to someone else talk with God can help you focus on Him.

Think of someone you know who talks about God's tangible presence in their life. Ask if you can pray together. While time alone with God is vital for spiritual growth:

*God Himself says that when two or more gather to focus on Him, something special happens (Matthew 18:20).*

If you are praying in public or with another person, remember to talk to God and not them. It's easy to fall into the trap of saying what you think another Christian wants to hear rather than what you need to communicate to God.

# PRIORITIES

*PRIORITIES are something that is more important than other things and that needs to be done or dealt with first.*

There are two types of priorities. Short-term priorities include your daily to-dos, such as tasks at school and home, finishing a report, or cooking dinner. However, long-term priorities, or life priorities, are the relationships and activities that make you happy — the things that really matter in life.

When we unpack priorities please understand that we will all have diverse priorities based on our values and belief systems. What helped me the most in this area was when I made a decision to understand that my values and beliefs don't always align with those closest to me however it was very vital that I stayed true to what was a priority in my life.

Often instead of exploring our own values, we default to the values of our family or culture. Take the time to consider what's important to you, what you stand for and what you believe in.

Avoid focusing on external rewards, such as "money, status or others' approval." Avoid "basing [your] priorities on what [you] believe [you] 'should' do."

To get what you want, you may need to set some goals. This is an effective way of making sure your priorities are achievable and getting to what's really important in your life.

Here are some questions that can help you think about your priorities:

- What are the big and small things that you want extra time for?
- How would you spend your time if you could clear your schedule, eliminate many day-to-day demands, and start over?
- Ask yourself, "Why is making these changes important to me?"

Think about how you could turn your number one priority, or "want," into a realistic and specific goal. For example, if spending more time with friends is very important to you, you might need to adjust how you spend your time overall and set a goal of seeing friends one evening each week.

Your goals and priorities may change over time as your life changes, but by revisiting the goals you've set, you'll be able to stay on track and make time for the things that are important to you. "Write down what you want to maintain, improve or change across the various domains of your well-being: relationships, health, finances, work, spirituality and personal life."

Priories effectively make your more productive and can help to reduce stress.

Please understand that everything can't be a TOP Priority.

## PEACE & POSIVIVITY

*Peace* and *Positivity* as defined in Chapter 3 are so valuable which explains why we much touch on it again briefly.

Some characteristics of a positive (peace) mindset are optimism, acceptance, resilience, gratitude, mindfulness and integrity.

Some simple tiny habits you can do for a positive peace mindset are:
- Telling yourself a few words of affirmation upon waking up in the morning
- Practicing mindfulness through a minute of deep breathing
- Accepting tiny things that you have no control over
- Break down daunting tasks to set small, attainable goals for yourself each day or week
- Keeping track of your accomplishments, no matter how small
- Journaling at least once per week to jot down thoughts, goals, blocks, and things you are grateful for, etc.

Adopting a positive peaceful mindset will overall improve and clear your headspace. Working on your mindset will also help you improve your coping skills, mental and physical health, as well as your critical thinking skills.

Where the positive peace mentality really comes into effect is beyond yourself; in order to affect sustainable positive peace in our societies and in the world, we must use our positive peace thinking to be creative and solve problems in our everyday life.

With the clarity that comes with this mentality, you will be able to productively and positively communicate your ideas with others, which allows for things such as: higher job satisfaction, productivity, efficiency and better interpersonal relationships.

Ultimately, the hope is that this clearer, positive peace headspace will lead to the cultivation of structures and changes that result in positive peace in your workplace, society, or beyond.

*"Nobody can bring you peace but yourself."* — *Ralph Waldo Emerson*

Embarking on a journey of self-discovery is similar to navigating through an uncharted wilderness. It requires resilience, patience, and an open heart. As you journey through the landscapes of your soul, remember to be kind to yourself, acknowledging that growth often comes from moments of discomfort and revelation. Embrace the multitude of emotions that accompany this expedition.

Along the way, you may encounter challenges that test your determination and moments of clarity that illuminate your path. Embrace both with grace and resilience, for growth often springs from adversity, and epiphanies often arise from moments of stillness. Allow yourself to feel every emotion that arises within you, for they are the colors that paint the canvas of your journey.

Surround yourself with individuals who empower and inspire you, but also cherish the moments of solitude that offer self-analysis and self-reflection. In the quiet whispers of your soul, deep truths are often revealed. Remember to document your revelations, whether through words, art, or any way that speaks to your spirit. These records will serve as indications of your evolution, guiding you back to your core when you lose your way.

As you progress on this expedition of self, embrace your authenticity with unwavering courage. Celebrate the the flaws, and the brilliance that make you uniquely you. Each step you take brings you closer to the masterpiece that is your true self — a mosaic of experiences, dreams, and aspirations waiting to be unveiled.

So, continue to explore, to grow, and to honor the journey you are on. Know that self-discovery is not a destination but a everlasting voyage — an ever-unfolding narrative of self-awareness and self-love. You are a work of art in progress, a masterpiece in the making. Embrace the beauty of your becoming and trust in the magic of your transformation.

As promised I have attached some additional writing space for your thoughts and reflections on what we have navigated through this book.

As you turn the pages of your journal, consider these guided questions to illuminate your thoughts, feelings, and experiences. Start by reflecting on what brought you to this moment: What are your current challenges, dreams, and goals? Delve into your daily life: What are you grateful for today? What lessons did the day bring? Explore your past: Which experiences have shaped you the most, and how? Look to the future: Where do you see yourself in five years, and what steps can you take to get there? Engage with your inner self: What are your core values, and are you living in alignment with them? These questions serve as a compass, guiding you through the rich landscape of your inner world, encouraging introspection, and fostering a deeper connection with yourself. Remember, there's no right or wrong way to journal. Let your thoughts flow freely, and embrace this journey of self-exploration with an open heart.

As you continue to journal, you may find that your writing evolves and reveals new insights about yourself. Allow your inner voice to speak authentically on the pages, without judgment or expectation. Your journal is a safe space to explore your thoughts, emotions, and aspirations. Embrace the process of self-discovery with curiosity and gentleness. Each entry is a step forward on your path to understanding, growth, and self-empowerment. By nurturing this practice, you cultivate a deeper connection with your innermost self and create a meaningful dialogue between your past, present, and future selves.

May your journaling journey be filled with moments of clarity, self-compassion, and personal transformation.

Embrace the power of your words and reflections as you embark on this voyage of self-exploration. Trust in the process, and allow the pages of your journal to become a mirror reflecting the beauty and complexity of your inner world. Happy journaling!

As we turn the final page of "Surviving You: A Journey of Self-Discovery," it is my hope that this book has served as a valuable tool on your path to self-awareness and growth. My deepest wish is that the insights and strategies shared within these pages continue to guide you long after you've put the book down, offering a source of support and inspiration whenever you need it most.

The journey towards becoming the best version of yourself is ongoing, and it's a path filled with challenges and obstacles.

Yet, the fact that you've purchased this book signifies your commitment to breaking free from the barriers you've set for yourself, stepping into a space of empowerment and self-love.

I am deeply thankful for the opportunity to have shared this journey with you, to have been a part of your process of transformation and self-discovery.

Remember, the journey to becoming a better you is a continuous one, but with each step forward, you are moving closer to a life where you no longer stand in your own way. Thank you for allowing me to be a part of your journey.

The kindest and warm regards,

Shateria Franklin

# The Surviving ME Journal

*"Every page of your journal is a canvas for your thoughts, where the ink becomes the mirror of your growth. Remember, the power of transformation lies within your story. Write not just to record, but to explore the depths of your soul and the heights of your dreams. Let each word guide you closer to the person you are meant to become."*

Made in the USA
Columbia, SC
17 June 2024

36737101R00057